Habib learns to say
Alhamdulillah

1 2 3 4 5 6 7 8 9 10

All rights reserved.
No part of this publication may be reproduced, stored in a retrieval system or transmitted in any form or by any means – electronic, mechanical, photocopying, recording or otherwise – without written permission from the publisher.

© Light Publishing 2018

Habib learns to say: Alhamdulillah
1st Edition

ISBN 978-1-915570-14-7
www.lightpublishing.co.uk

Habib and Omar are eating at their Grandma's house.

They've eaten all their beans!

Now, they can go and play.

"Omar, you forgot to say

Alhamdulillah!"

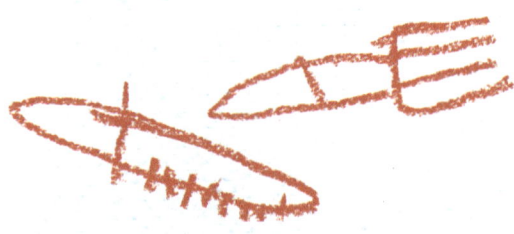

Habib is crying because he fell off the slide.

Dad is wiping his tears and making him feel better. Very quickly, Habib's pain is gone. "Is that better, Habib?"

"Yes, that's better.

Alhamdulillah!"

Today, it's Eid.

Yippee! Habib and Layla have received lots of presents. They are very pleased.

"Are you happy, children?"

"Yes, **Alhamdulillah!** Thank you, Allah!"

Habib is sick. He's coughing a lot.

Luckily, Mum's there. She looks after Habib and stays by his side.

"**Alhamdulillah**

I've got a mummy who loves me and takes care of me!"

Dad takes Habib to the amusement park. Habib has a great time. He goes on all the rides and he even gets to have an ice cream. Habib really has a lovely day.

"**Alhamdulillah** for this day!"

Your turn to play!

Try to guess…

In which picture does Habib look like he is saying

Alhamdulillah?

Answer: 1

أَلْحَمْدُ لِلّٰهِ

الْحَمْدُ لِلَّهِ